IN THE FOREST

LOOK ONCE LOOK AGAIN

For a free color catalog describing Gareth Stevens Publishing's list of high-quality books and multimedia programs, call 1-800-542-2595 (USA) or 1-800-461-9120 (Canada). Gareth Stevens Publishing's Fax: (414) 225-0377.
See our catalog, too, on the World Wide Web: gsinc.com

Library of Congress Cataloging-in-Publication Data

Schwartz, David M.
   In the forest / by David M. Schwartz; photographs by Dwight Kuhn.
       p. cm. — (Look once, look again)
     Includes bibliographical references (p. 23) and index.
     Summary: Introduces, in simple text and photographs, the characteristics of some of
the animals and plants that can be found in the forest. Includes a chipmunk, box turtle,
fern, bull moose, moth, ermine, and white birch.
     ISBN 0-8368-2222-6 (lib. bdg.)
     1. Forest animals—Juvenile literature. 2. Forest plants—Juvenile literature. [1. Forest
animals. 2. Forest plants.] I. Kuhn, Dwight, ill. II. Title. III. Series: Schwartz, David M.
Look once, look again.
QL112.S395   1998
591.73—dc21   98-15396

This North American edition first published in 1998 by
Gareth Stevens Publishing
1555 North RiverCenter Drive, Suite 201
Milwaukee, Wisconsin 53212 USA

First published in the United States in 1997 by Creative Teaching Press, Inc., P. O. Box 6017, Cypress, California, 90630-0017.

Printed in the United States of America

1 2 3 4 5 6 7 8 9 02 01 00 99 98

FOREST

A SPRINGBOARDS INTO
SCIENCE
SERIES

Gareth Stevens Publishing
MILWAUKEE

by David M. Schwartz
photographs by Dwight Kuhn

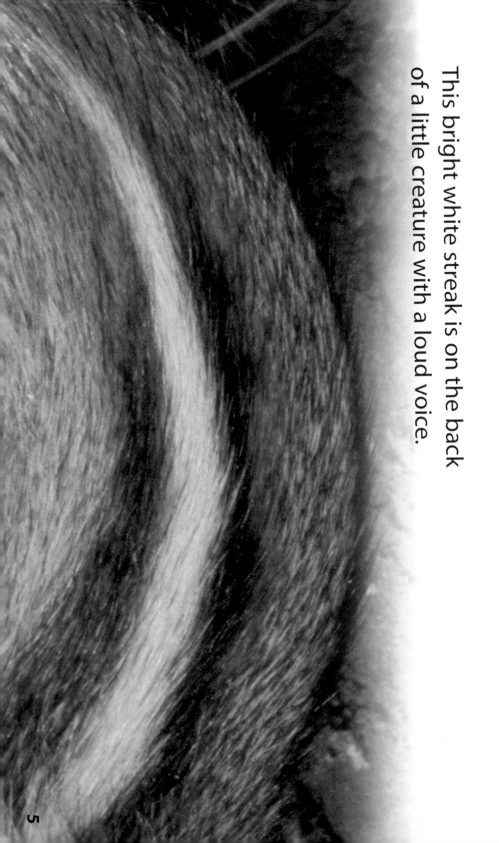

This bright white streak is on the back of a little creature with a loud voice.

In summer and fall, chipmunks busily gather food. They carry nuts, seeds, and fruit in their cheek pouches. Then they bury the food in underground dens.

A chipmunk's den has many little rooms. Some are for sleeping, and some are for storing food. When winter comes, the chipmunk eats the hidden food.

If you get too close to this scaly leg, it will disappear inside a shell!

This is a box turtle.
When scared, a box turtle
pulls itself into its shell,
tight as a box.
Some people
keep box turtles
as pets. These
turtles can live
forty years
or more.

These are not little eggs of a creepy-crawly.
They are from a plant that carpets the forest floor.

Ferns have tiny, brown spheres underneath their leafy parts. They are called "spore cases." When the cases are ripe, millions of tiny spores fly away with the wind. Some land nearby, and some travel very far. A few will grow into new ferns.

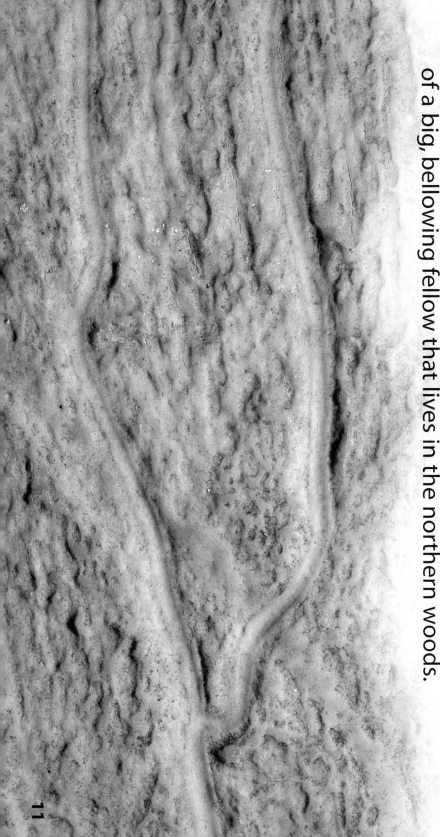

Is this part of a tree? Is it part of a rock? No, it is from the head of a big, bellowing fellow that lives in the northern woods.

11

A bull moose wears a crown of antlers. In the summertime, these antlers are covered with soft, furry skin called "velvet." In the fall, the velvet falls off. The hard, bony antlers will soon fall off, too. Next spring, the bull moose will grow new antlers. They will be even bigger than this year's antlers.

This looks feathery, but it is not from a bird.
It belongs to an animal that flutters around at night.

It is an antenna on a colorful cecropia moth. The male moth has two feathery antennae. He uses them like a nose. A male moth can sense female moths, by smell, from 3 miles (5 kilometers) away!

What is at the other end of this black-tipped tail?

15

It is an ermine, or short-tailed weasel. In the summer, an ermine's fur is dark. By winter, the ermine turns snow white, except for its black-tipped tail. Why do you think an ermine changes its coat?

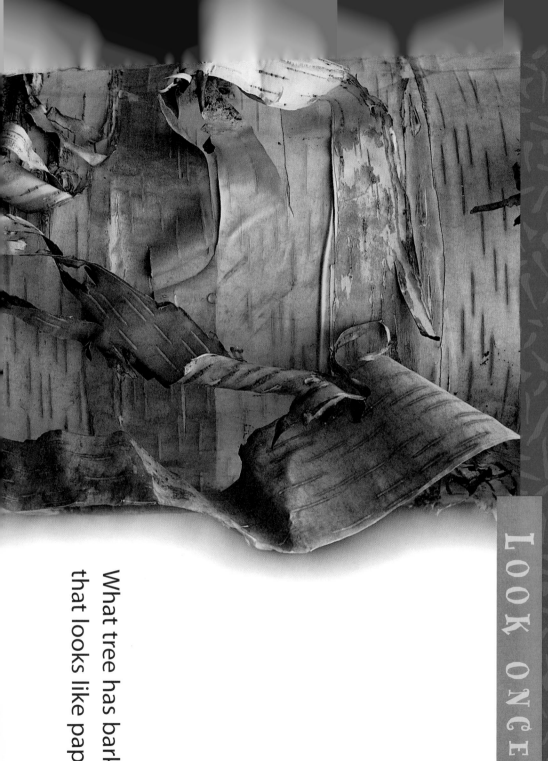

What tree has bark
that looks like paper?

17

A white birch is also called a "paper birch." You can see why! Years ago, American Indians used papery birch bark to make canoes.

Birch bark has many layers. The outer layers peel naturally, but the inner layers make a tight seal around the tree's trunk. Never peel a birch's bark because you might harm its "skin." If water and insects get in, they also harm the tree.

Look closely. Can you name these plants and animals?

LOOK AGAIN

A.

Chipmunk

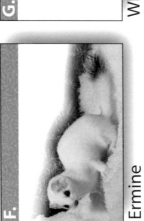

B.

Box turtle

C.

Fern

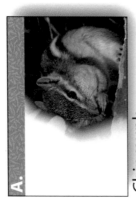

D.

Bull moose

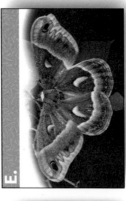

E.

Cecropia moth

F.

Ermine

G.

White birch

How many were you able to identify correctly?

antenna: one of the thin organs on the head of an insect or other animal that is used for touching and smelling.

antler: a bony growth on the head of some animals, such as moose and deer.

bellowing: making a load, roaring sound.

box turtle: a type of turtle that can pull its head and legs into its shell so tightly that its body is like a closed-up box.

den: the home or shelter of a wild animal, sometimes in a hole or cave.

ermine: a short-tailed weasel that has white winter fur.

fern: a plant with feathery leaves that reproduces by sending out spores.

pouch: the part of an animal's body that is like a bag to hold something, such as the cheeks of a chipmunk.

scaly: covered with small, thin, platelike parts. Turtles and snakes have scaly skin.

sphere: a round or ball-shaped object.

spore: a single plant cell that grows into a new plant.

spore case: a container for the spores of a plant.

velvet: the soft skin that covers and feeds the growing antlers of some animals, such as moose or deer.

weasel: a woodland animal with soft fur and a long, narrow body.

ACTIVITIES

Forest in a Fishbowl

Put a layer of gravel or pebbles in the bottom of a fishbowl. Add several inches (centimeters) of potting soil, and pat the soil lightly. Plant ferns, moss, and other forest plants. Gently water your forest and cover it with plastic wrap, leaving a small opening at one edge. Place the fishbowl in a sunny window, and add water as needed to keep the soil moist.

All in the Family

The ermine is just one member of the weasel family. There are many other interesting members, including the otter and the mink. From library books and the Internet, find out about other types of weasels and where they live. How are the the various types in this family similar? How are they different?

Wrap It Up!

Make your own "woodsy" wrapping paper using leaves you collect. Cover a work area with newspaper, and then carefully paint one side of a leaf with poster paint. Press the painted side of the leaf onto a piece of plain paper. Carefully lift up the leaf and repeat to make multiple prints. Add paint to the leaf whenever necessary for the effect you want. When the decorated paper dries, use it to wrap a gift!

Winter White

Do a simple experiment to learn about camouflage. With a hole puncher, make dots from different colors of paper, including white. Scatter the paper dots onto a piece of white paper. Which dots are easiest to see? Which are the hardest to see?

More Books to Read

Animal Survival (series). Michel Barré (Gareth Stevens)

Butterflies and Moths. Jim Feltwell (Dorling Kindersley)

Exploring Forests. Eco-Journey (series). Barbara J. Behm and Veronica Bonar (Gareth Stevens)

Moose Magic for Kids. Animal Magic for Kids (series). Jeff Fair (Gareth Stevens)

Squirrels and Chipmunks. Allan Fowler (Childrens Press)

A Tree in a Forest. Jan Thornhill (Simon & Schuster)

Young Naturalist Field Guides (series). (Gareth Stevens)

Videos

The Tree: A Living Community. (Churchill Media)

Tree-Living Animals. (Wood Knapp Video)

What Good Are Woods? (Agency for Instructional Technology)

Web Sites

www.nationalgeographic.com/main.html

www.arborday.com/

Some web sites stay current longer than others. For further web sites, use your search engines to locate the following topics: *antlers, ferns, forests, moose, moths, trees, turtles,* and *weasels.*

Index